The Nomenclature of Small Things

The Nomenclature of
Small Things

Lynn Pedersen

Carnegie Mellon University Press
Pittsburgh 2016

Acknowledgments

Grateful acknowledgment is made to the editors of the following publications in which these poems appeared:

Borderlands: "The Mier Expedition: The Drawing of the Black Bean by Frederic Remington (1896)"; *The Chattahoochee Review:* "Miscarriage," "At Forty"; *Cider Press Review:* "Still Life," "How to Move Away," "Correction," "Eve Paints the Apple Tree," "Begin"; *The Comstock Review:* "The Rift," "The Sterility of Numbers," "The Infinite Density of Grief," "The Second Son," "Pre-Op," "After Seven Months, Alaskans Begin to Bury Their Dead"; *Ecotone:* "On Reading about the Illness and Death of Darwin's Daughter Annie"; *Ellipsis:* "The Birth of Superstition," "Hangman"; *Heron Tree:* "Wilson's Warbler," "A Catalog of What We're Not Meant to See"; *Little Patuxent Review:* "Isaac Newton Waits Out the Plague"; *Nassau Review:* "Sugar in Space"; *New England Review:* "How to Speak Nineteenth Century"; *Slipstream:* "Decay" *Southern Poetry Review:* "Horse Latitudes"; *Sow's Ear Poetry Review:* "I hate Darwin"

Several of the poems in this collection not published in journals are published in the chapbooks *Theories of Rain* (Main Street Rag, 2009) and *Tiktaalik, Adieu* (Finishing Line Press, 2014).

"Why We Speak English" was featured on NPR's *The Writer's Almanac* in March 2009, and appears in *Stone, River, Sky: An Anthology of Georgia Poems* from Negative Capability Press, 2015.

"Platypus: Hoax" is published in the anthology *Other Countries: Contemporary Poets Rewiring History*, edited by Claire Trévien and Gareth Prior, from Inpress Books, 2014.

"Something about Darwin" and "A Brief History of the Passenger Pigeon" are featured in the anthology *[Ex]tinguished & [Ex]tinct: An Anthology of Things That No Longer [Ex]ist*, published by Twelve Winters Press, 2014.

Book design: Connie Amoroso

Library of Congress Control Number 2015945714
ISBN 978-0-88748-609-8
Copyright © 2016 by Lynn Pedersen
All rights reserved
Printed and bound in the United States of America

Contents

Catalog I.

11   The Infinite Density of Grief
12   The Birth of Superstition
13   Nomenclature: The First Day
14   Miscarriage
15   Eve Paints the Apple Tree
17   The Sterility of Numbers
18   How to Speak Nineteenth Century
19   A Catalog of What We're Not Meant to See
21   The Rift
22   Isaac Newton Waits Out the Plague
24   Wilson's Warbler
26   *The Mier Expedition: The Drawing of the Black Bean* by Frederic Remington (1896)
28   How to Move Away
30   Something about Darwin

Catalog II.

33   Begin
34   After Seven Months, Alaskans Begin to Bury Their Dead
35   A Brief History of the Passenger Pigeon
36   Pre-Op
37   Taxonomy: Taxidermy
38   Correction
39   Platypus: Hoax
41   Decay
42   Found Poem: Sir Hamon L'Estrange Gives the Only Documented Account of a Living Dodo in Britain, 1638
43   What the Frog's Eye Tells the Frog's Brain
44   Pond

45   Hangman

47   I hate Darwin

48   Horse Latitudes

49   Grief and Geometry

51   Primer

52   What Is Still, What Is Moving

Catalog III.

55   The Classification of Impermanence

57   The Second Son

58   Braids

60   Ballast

62   Still Life

63   My Grandmother Peels Apples for Sauce

64   Why We Speak English

66   The Quick of Things

67   Selling Skies at the Soho Bazaar, 1790

68   At Forty

69   Darwin's Twin Sister

70   Sugar in Space

72   On Reading about the Illness and Death of Darwin's
        Daughter Annie

73   A Way with Words

74   Dickinsonia

77   Notes

Thou hast clothed me with skin and flesh,
and hast fenced me with bones and sinews.

—Job 10:11

Catalog I.

The Infinite Density of Grief

What no one tells you is grief
has properties: expands like a gas
to fill space and time—the four corners
of your room, the calendar
with its boxed days—
and when you think it can't claim anything more,
collapses in on itself, a dying star,
compacting until not even a thimble
of light escapes.

Then grief sleeps, becomes
the pebble in your shoe you can almost
ignore, until a penny on a sidewalk,
dew on a leaf—
some equation detailing the relationship
between loss and minutiae
sets the whole in motion again—

your unborn child, folded and folded
into a question, or the notes
you passed in grade school
with their riddles—
*What kind of room
has no windows or doors?*

The Birth of Superstition

It's not hard to imagine: my ancestor—a dry season,
    dust like chalk on her tongue—mixes
        spit with clay,

traces a river on rock. Next day: rain.

           Why shouldn't she believe
    in the power of rock and her own hand?

I carry this need for pattern and rule, to see connections
    where there aren't necessarily any.

          After my first miscarriage,
I cut out soda, cold cuts.

    After the second, vacuuming and air travel.

After the third—it's chalk and spit again. I circle rocks,
    swim the icy river.

        And when my son is born, he balances
the chemical equation that is this world.

           And logic?

Logic is my son's kite, good so long as you have
    wind, string,

        something heavier than hope

          to tether you.

Nomenclature: The First Day

It comes down to what Adam could sort by eye,
by hand: fire, sun,

or ants, crickets (he overlooks plankton),
                    Eve whispering suggestions in his ear—

dragonfly, black widow.

The sea creatures must have been the worst, their constant
schooling, and then their shells—digging into the pliant arches

of the feet. And did Adam weigh the goodness
of things in his hands? Stop to admire the beetle?

Of course there's no name for death,
the absence of—

because no Cain and no Abel.

And there's no name for the smallest of spaces,
like between fitted stones, gaps between want and expectation,

hesitations between breaths, the escape
of air between the teeth when the mouth forms

yes. Adam lies on his back on a stone and names the clouds
after the whitest down and the fastest bird,

and still no syllables on his tongue for the small
of Eve's back, the rush of plums,

the film of salt on his temples.

Miscarriage

Nothing to do but return
to the apartment, cross the green
threshold, wedding gifts barely
three months out of their wrappings.

It was the plates that angered me most,
round like ova, fragile,
bleached like bones. I longed to take
each onto the small side porch,
smash it to atoms with a hammer—
one blow to the center—
repeat until I was squatting in a beach
of porcelain ground to a fine sand,
my knees bleeding.
Who's to say all sand isn't born
of grief?

If I whittle myself down
to marrow, nucleus, mitochondrion—
What's the right word
for the smallest pocket of self?
Soul? Essence? Seed
you grieve in your hand?

Eve Paints the Apple Tree

after lines from Cesare Pavese's "Grappa in September"

Her problem, of course, is that she was never a child,
and so hadn't the opportunity

to know the tree as a sapling, to climb
its branches, bark roughing her thighs, but only

viewed it with the distance of an adult.
Now it's a question of staying on task with the story

of suffering a great pain. To climb
perhaps another higher tree,

and look back into Eden at the lost crown,
to paint what she remembers later

of that last day: the sky's blue witness, the leaves slick, glistening.
And the snake—had the snake not spoken? Was it

her imagination, trick of the shadows?
She must variegate the color of bark: siennas, umbers,

ochers, reds, even green moss. Branches
may break off during their lifespans,

may be riddled with knots, regrets.
Cover her right eye and look with the left,

then reverse: each eye sees color differently.
How does she paint the temptation? Every limb and leaf

of before and after? The fulcrum where *everything
stops to ripen*? Regret a tart yellow.

Black for secrets. Her children must know that the ochers and umbers even now conceal *fruit that would fall at a touch*.

The Sterility of Numbers

One out of ten pregnancies ends
this way—

as if I could conceive one-tenth of a child,
view loss as a fraction.

—and the chance of it happening again
is like lightning striking twice.

A voice whispers
near my ear—

There was probably something
terribly wrong.

Alone in a flood
of fluorescence, I stare

at the screen,
the tiny white form curled

into itself, pressing up
against the glass

like a moth resting
on a windowpane

because it sees light.

How to Speak Nineteenth Century

Forget about the nomenclature
of the moon: lunar impact craters, rilles; your voice
translated into fiber optics or beamed pinpoint to pinpoint
on the planet. Here, all words are spoken to someone's face.
Earth. Seeds. Thresher. Plow. Timber'd.

                                                So unnerving, you say,
having to look someone that long in the eye, just speaking
your mind. Or too involved, in the first place,
the five-mile walk to your friend's house,
your skirt catching on the field grass.

You need to know not hydrogen, oxygen, H_2O, but
water: where to find it, how to dig
for it, how to keep a well from running dry.

Not chlorophyll and photosynthesis,
the word is *harvest*—the hard "t"
uncompromising as hunger—

sunup and *sundown*, light.
Forget meteorology, you need to know
bird migration, insect hatches, animal hibernation—
what the falling leaves tell you.
When the blossoms of the apple tree fall, plant corn. In short,

the world is still whole to you.
                        Each molecule. Each syllable. Each grain.

A Catalog of What We're Not Meant to See

> *"Goethe demanded that science should always hold to the human scale.*
> *He opposed the use of the microscope, since he believed that what cannot be*
> *seen with the naked eye should not be seen, and that what is hidden from*
> *us is hidden for a purpose."*
>
> —John Banville, *Science*

If something is hidden from us for a purpose, no wonder
this feeling of always having lost something or someone,
of satisfaction or completion just
around the corner or under the pillows
or between the floorboards, something
escaping us in the wind.

Pocked edge of a razor, raw weave of linen or silk,
sparks struck from flint or steel,
six-branched figures formed on the surface of urine by freezing,
the stinging tips of nettles.

And the minute bodies that live among us: mites, a louse, a flea,
the beard of a wild oat,
teeth of a snail, wings of a fly,
the eggs of silkworms,
blue mold.

We're left with what's immediately above and below
and around us—bulk of table and chair.

Though as years go on . . . you find less
and less it's things that you want, that you believe in.
Instead, it's departure and return: the slip of winter.

No wonder Robert Hooke (no friend of Goethe's)
built a telescope as high as a house
to make up for man's meek senses, discovered

seventy-eight stars in the Pleiades cluster,
more than twice as many as Galileo had counted.

What Goethe especially hated
was Hooke's fibrillar structure of cells, the hollowness of cork:
its series of tiny boxes that imply
what holds us together is nothing.

The Rift

Three months now I've been waiting
for your letter. And today, I discover
Madagascar—how it was torn away from Africa
sixty-five million years ago
and the gap
filled with water.
The same thing is happening
in the Great Rift Valley.
You can't see the seam
beneath the grass, but the land imperceptibly
strains north and east,
inching towards the Indian Ocean.

The animals don't know,
or if they know, don't seem to care.
A bird bends its head,
scratches the ground.
Shadows of trees grow longer,
rotate around trunks
like sundials.

And I imagine evolution—how amphibians
used to be fish, grew legs
and lungs—
branched off.

Isaac Newton Waits Out the Plague

When plague closed Cambridge University in 1665, twenty-two-year-old Isaac Newton returned to his widowed mother's home. During these eighteen months, he formulated his theories of gravitation and motion, conducted experiments with optics and developed infinitesimal calculus.

You court the ellipse. Spend your nights
looking in mirrors. Keep a list of your sins.

Only someone confined could envision the moon
as torn between escaping on a trajectory into space
and falling. How it must have been

to feel the universe converging
in one's mind to a pinpoint. To see it all, finally,
as would a God.

So many people dying and yet, these
your best years. What mechanism
coerces the mockingbird back
and back again to your window?
Surely the equation exists?

Apothecaries in their bird masks
hawk their plague cures, beaks
stuffed with herbs to ward off the stench, the miasmas.

What good does it do to postulate
that the sun's density is one-quarter of the earth's
when the next village over, its mass,
its whole populace is waning? The healthy
quarantined at home with their ill. Who knew

the moon and calculus needed one another?

Perhaps it's a romantic notion—confinement
and discovery. I'd like to think if I shut myself
away for as many months I'd come up
with more than scraps of paper folded into birds.

The plague abates, and you labor
at your telescope, diagrams, papers. Battle
your fear—not of death or boils, or bruises
blooming under the skin—but of
never finishing as the moon slips away.

Wilson's Warbler

"I shall at least leave a small beacon to point out where I perished."
—Alexander Wilson, speaking of his ornithology

Like children divvying up marbles,

Linnaeus claims the plants, his friend Peter Artedi
the fishes,

        and decades later, Alexander Wilson,
North American birds, *their habits and habitats, as if they were companions.*

A schema on which to hang every species. Thistle, poison ivy

pose no problems,

but birds and fish are another story:

Artedi, in spite of his love of the sea, anglers and pufferfish,
drowns at thirty in an Amsterdam canal, and Wilson succumbs
to dysentery, though myth has it

he drowned in a river
in pursuit of a bird. *The irony*

of some stories is their truncation.
And Wilson's promise (years before he died)
that he would continue his quest *even if it killed him*—

        as if the Black
Throated Bunting thirsted in its dry meadowlands and canary grass
for categorization, not wanting to be mistaken
as it is—its flight and notes—for the Corn Bunting of Europe.

All along it's Wilson who doesn't want to be mistaken, *subsumed*. Birds named after him,

rather than sons.

The Mier Expedition: The Drawing of the Black Bean by Frederic Remington (1896)

During the days of the Republic of Texas, the Mier Expedition was the last, and the most disastrous, of the raiding expeditions from Texas into Mexico. On March 25, 1843, the 176 prisoners of the Mier Expedition were forced to draw from a jar containing 159 white beans and 17 black beans; those drawing a black bean would be shot.

It hardly seems spring, not a lick
of green in the courtyard.

No shackles, but it's the math
one can't escape: the problem of
how to differentiate color without sight—
perhaps the black beans slicker, the white
softer to the fingernail,

and this déjà vu: my aunt's cancer,
news reports of wars, car accidents,
this feeling that something's
being doled out, luck or fate
without equal chances, the black beans
we draw in our sleep. Or are we
awake, each day arm-deep in the vessel
with this illusion of choice, wondering
how each outcome would taste if
rolled on the tongue?

The grid of the courtyard and the arches
only tease; this geometry, this symmetry isn't for us.
We start each day blind. There's no logic

to what happens. The men in line know this,
some of them joking, some staring
at their feet, just wanting to go home.

How to Move Away

It's best to wake early, four, five a.m., while
the neighbors sleep and the moon floats
like a pearl in a pool of ink. In half-light
the empty house is less familiar, less sad—the walls
with their nail holes, the carpet—its patterns of wear,
curtains with no job to do. I sit
on my suitcase, eat powdered donuts;
a napkin for a plate, juice out of a paper cup.
Make one last check of the cupboards,
the drawers. Run my hand along
the countertops, the stair rail, trace
the walls with my fingertips, each scar
proof of my childhood, my initials
carved into the tree of this, our sixth house.

My family could write a *Handbook for Leaving*—
the way we pack up during summer solstice,
disconnect from people and places like an abrupt
shutting off of electricity. My father's convinced himself
that the unknown is always better, the way the retina sees
images upside down and the brain corrects.

                              Here I smoked
candy cigarettes, my breath in winter passing
for smoke, pale green of my bedroom. I counted
the number of intersections on the way to school (four).
I bundle memories together, weight them with stones
like unwanted kittens drowned in a creek.

What kind of animal constantly moves?
The point of migration is the return.
We're nomads without the base knowledge

of where to find water. These moves are
like arranged marriages; economics now,
love later. Maybe it's not against nature
to move. Most of the body is no more
than ten years old and blood renews itself
every 90 days. But leaving disturbs the fabric
of a place. I'd rather stay and witness change.
My mother always wanting to plant perennials
that we never stay to see. I pour some water
on the marigolds clattering around the mailbox,
Aztec flowers of death, their strong scent
a beacon to lost souls. Then we drive away,
the blank windows like the blank eyes of
the dead, waiting for someone to seal the past with a penny.

Something about Darwin

Most of earth's animals have become extinct: moas, mammoths,
ammonites, mastodons, saber-toothed cats. If anyone

should understand such loss it's Darwin—
cartographer of tails and limbs. Permian

to Triassic. Mesozoic to Cenozoic. Epochs and eras.
But this is abstraction, like political boundaries on a map

or saying Monday bleeds into Tuesday
and Monday is gone (gone where?),

and what happened to Monday's sound, its light?

What's tangible is the space left:
fossil footprints, my fingers fit the grooves

of Cambrian seas, rocky joists, my knuckles
dovetail Jurassic backbones.

But there is no account in the *Origin of Species*
of grief. No Cretaceous eulogy. No prediction that 300 million years

after the trilobites I should mourn the loss
of any of these. Is it only tragic when the last

of a species dies? How about the first born? The ones sited in the middle
in strata of rock or ancient sands?

Where have they gone? Who grieves for them?

Catalog II.

Begin

No plans and preparations without first
having a vision, like an angel appearing to you
in your bedchamber, or thought slipping in
as you butter your toast, stir your coffee. And how
to know what to pack, especially for a trip to where
no one's ever been? Easier to follow
a river or a mountain range. I've read
there are few new roads, that most roads
follow common paths, follow the route
animals have taken, as if the animals know
the easiest grade to follow, the path of water,
and the Oregon Trail is just a dot to dot
of Indian footpaths—so Lewis and Clark,
or some other explorers, can't take credit.
And particularly difficult is the journey
to a place that never existed—the Fountain of Youth.
How do you map that? What part of a mountain range,
what river corresponds to fantasy? Beginning
is the hardest part, the part that unlike the vision
takes action. It takes loading the wagon,
telling the relatives goodbye,
packing ammunition. You can never be sure
what you will need, and so the Oregon Trail is littered—
trunks, clothes, pianos, chairs, silverware—
anything to lighten the load
before crossing the mountains. In any journey,
there is a time when you have to ditch the sick
horse, the cumbersome companion—the naysayers.
It's all about getting somewhere
(and maybe back again) with your hide intact. Otherwise,
there's no one to tell the story.

After Seven Months, Alaskans Begin to Bury Their Dead

Memorial Day before one can dig down six feet—

It has nothing to do with you, what the earth wants
or doesn't, turning its winter shoulder on you.

Maybe the dead don't mind being in limbo, waiting
to be interred, icicles, I imagine,

in their hair. But the living mind, and want to go on
with their planting, their plans,

like the Athabascan woman
who buried her mother using fire
to thaw the ground, seeming to know

how to speak with the earth, knead
the earth with fire. Or the Inuit

burying their dead under piles of stone. The rest of us—
knocking with no answer. Or worse,

using dynamite in old mining towns
to carve out winter graves. It's hard

to break ground to do anything.

A Brief History of the Passenger Pigeon

Not to be confused with messenger pigeons, birds sent behind
enemy lines in war, but think passengers as in birds carrying suitcases,
sharing a berth on a train, or traveling in bamboo cages on a ship,
always migrating on a one-way to extinction. How would extinction
look on a graph? A steady climb, or a plateau, then a precipitous cliff
at the dawn of humans?

Nesting grounds eight hundred square miles in area. Skies swollen
with darkening multitudes. Days and days of unbroken flocks passing
over. *Ectopistes migratorius.*

And the last of the species, Martha, named for Martha Washington,
dies in a cage in 1914 at the Cincinnati Zoo.

Forget clemency. We are the worst kind of predator, not even
deliberate in our destruction. Our killing happens à la carte, on the
side (*side of Dodo?*).

And because the nineteenth century did not enlist a battlefield artist
for extinctions, there are no official witnesses to the slaughter, just
participants. If you could somehow travel back to this scene, through
the would-be canvas, you would run flailing your arms toward the
hardwood forests and the men with sticks and guns and boiling
sulphur pots to bring birds out of the trees, as if you could deliver
50,000 individual warnings, or throw yourself prostrate on the
ground, as if your one body could hold sway.

Pre-Op

I should meditate on the tympanic membrane,
present tense of the inner ear, not social studies
films; the crane outside the window echoing
Brasilia, how Dom Bosco had a vision
and next thing, a field in South America's sheared
of trees, patterned and gridded with dirt roads
like runways and a skeleton
of a cathedral rising like a crown of ribs.

Or the *Gunsmith of Williamsburg*. Not the part
where it takes two men six days to hammer and file
the barrel, widen it with linseed oil
and an army of bits, but the part about forging
the lock and trigger: each piece notched, coaxed
into interlocking shapes held by pins, the intricacy
of a watch or an ear. And how the gunsmith
takes the time to engrave the brass with scrolls, flowers,
vines. Some beautiful offering.

It's 1:30 p.m. The surgeon arrives with a blue pen
to mark my son's right ear—the ear that 200 years ago
would have gone deaf, missed the pitch
of file on metal. Strange how one can measure time
not by what's passed, but by
what's left: a pile of iron shavings,
wick of a candle, the smallest sound.

Taxonomy: Taxidermy

Audubon paints stuffed birds;
Darwin nets and shoots specimens
all over Galapagos before
returning on the *Beagle*. How to
wrap one's logic around
kill first: categorize later,
the naturalists
doing both deeds?

Taxonomy crafts order out of clutter
or the proverbial chaos. Everything
in its place. Taxidermy is everything
in its pride. Displaying the kill.
Taxi: arrangement, a buffet of marble-eyed
deer heads on a wall.

Does the taxidermist care
what kingdom, phylum, class
the specimen (or he) comes from?
A mnemonic: *King Phillip Can Order the Fish Guest Special.*
What's the difference between
an individual who mounts animal heads
and a field biologist
who collects butterflies only to display them
driven through with pins?

One mucks about in a ditch in search
of species that inhabit tall grasses
and one goes about his methodical
pick, piece, and place. Stuff and dust.
Hang death on the wall.
The gathering: the dusting.

Correction

When I wrote the poem about the Great Rift Valley,
what I should have said
was that the valley floor had been under strain
for some time; in fact, for thousands of years
before I was born, and the escarpments
had always been there.
It wasn't my place to appropriate a valley's grief (or its length)—
the elephants, the rhinos hunted to near extinction.
The elephants learning not to trumpet
to avoid being killed. Seven lakes
with no outlet to the sea.

                              I could have chosen
not to wait for the mail, or to attach such
significance to a lone postcard from Donegal, Ireland,
picture of a man watching a sunset.

It wasn't geography that failed me, but
language. My attempts to decode.
When I was eight, I never listened to my father
deliver his sermons from the pulpit. I took
the Sunday program and filled in all the empty letters,
and I did the same with the postcard
from Ireland—filled in
between the words *hello* and *take care*.

Platypus:Hoax

"A degree of fcepticifm is not only pardonable, but laudable; and I ought perhaps to acknowledge that I almoft doubt the teftimony of my own eyes with refpect to the ftructure of this animal's beak."
—George Shaw, 1799

Duck beak, beaver body, head of a quadruped,
otter in miniature. Pelt has to be sewn, stitches
hidden somewhere in the fur
in this bird-reptile-mammal,
this taxidermist's joke. Who blames

a man for doubting the testimony of his senses?
Like the arctic expeditioners who, seeing
no houses or trees by which to judge size or distance, mistook
a hare for a polar bear.

What to call this creature: watermole, duckbill, duckmole?

No one in the eighteenth century suspects
that our *Homo sapiens* brains are a hodgepodge
of jellyfish-lizard-mouse,

or that our ribs, wrists, necks carry the story
of how we descended from *Tiktaalik,*
ancient fish (not a fish or a tetrapod
but a fishapod) transitioning sea to land,
always this moving and adapting. And loss, the loss
of the bony operculum behind the skull means
we have a neck, a head that moves independently
of our body, and the growth of land bones (ribs, limbs)
sets us free of water.

At the first platypus dissection, Everard Home slits the animal
from the extra bones of its shoulder girdle to the roots

of its claws. No doubts now. No doubts
as to the creature's genuine nature. Unlike our tongues,
our animal bodies—our skeletons cannot lie.

Decay

Uptick in grittiness. A slight yellowing.
Not much to notice at first but paint flaking off faded siding
and settling on grass like unseasonable snow.

Why is the direction of decay always down?
Down the direction that boards hang. Rooflines droop
like the backs of old mares as gravity takes its toll.
Fall leaves transposed to a fine dust of cinnamon. Down

is in the earth, is where ancients are buried, is the direction
birds land to feed on carrion. Your job
is to fight this loosening of pattern, slackness
in the ropes, to build up bridges,

cliff houses. Taking off (birth) requires more
energy, but landing (death) more skill. At a certain point,
decay has nothing more to do with hunger. You move past
hunger, the earth's slow digestion.

The softer objects yield first: flesh, plants, the cell wall,
the plaster wall. Teeth last longest
in the fossil record. The earth cupping your spine, cradling
your skull in the blessing you always resisted.

Found Poem: Sir Hamon L'Estrange Gives the Only Documented Account of a Living Dodo in Britain, 1638

"Driven to extinction: Who killed the Dodo?"
—The Independent

It was kept in a chamber, and was a great fowle
somewhat bigger than the largest Turkey Cock, and so legged
and footed, but stouter and thicker
and of a more erect shape, coloured before like the breast
of a young cock fesan, and on the back
a dunn or deare colour. The keeper called it
a Dodo, and in the ende of a chymney
in the chamber there lay a heape
of large pebble stones, wherof hee gave it
many in our sight, some as big as nutmegs,
and the keeper told us she eats them (conducing to digestion).

What the Frog's Eye Tells the Frog's Brain

from a course in Practical Thinking, The Open University

Movement in relation to background—size, darkness of objects
count, *the frog's brain functioning in layers, one part*
responding to fixed patterns
of light and shade (features of the pond), while another
notes fast-moving forms (insects the frog eats),
while another part of the brain perceives
slow-moving patterns (larger animals that eat frogs). I understand

this—say, a fly, a pinprick darts
against grass: ganglia fire—motion and speed
in relation to background, not unlike
my neighbor's cat, ghosting past my patio door,

or the lizards that make their way like smoky die-cuts
across my carpet. Anything catches my eye:
bicyclist, bird of my peripheral
vision. This isn't

knowledge, something I was taught, that speed
and shadow equal predator or prey—
though the startle response is still there,

that quickening. I'm no better.

Pond

for my aunt

I half expect to hear her voice
among the tattered reeds,

the lady's smock and meadowsweet
ignorant of her
skill with petunias.

At family gatherings, we circle
folding chairs, cast a net
for some story about her as if
the past could be lured
like a fish to bait.

We've no control over what rises to the surface
or what propels it.

Every story ends
with winter.

We fatten ourselves on the bank,
remember the fable of the ant—the grasshopper
winter-hungry.

It is best to prepare.

I reach down and through
my own shadow—
darter nymphs, minnows, the entire underworld
skitters away.

Hangman

It wasn't clear what the argument
was about, but it began

and ended with words,
you loaning me the *Dictionary*

of Classical Mythology in September,
and by finals

the challenge of Hangman
like a duel. Just nineteen,

what could we have known
of love? For you it was kiss

for kiss, a commodity
exchange, game theory,

sky, phlegm, fjord, buxom,
your delight in drawing head,

neck, torso, limbs,
fingers (to be kind)

all those parts
you used to caress.

I could only counter with
rivers: *Yukon, Yangtze, Styx,*

the scale always tipping in your favor,
your better vocabulary,

your disbelief that I couldn't
have guessed *myrrh*—

and your anger,
all talons and feathers,

like a hawk
blaming the field mouse

for falling victim,
then resenting the emptiness

of the field.

I hate Darwin

for being the first to point out it was inevitable,
my loss, shoving it in my face at a low
point in my grief, his mechanics of extinction,
charts and diagrams of finches' beaks,
miscellaneous islands, the non-fixed nature of species.

For asking the wrong questions: not
why so many variations? Not why birds off the coast
of South America resemble the birds of that continent,
while birds off the coast of Africa mirror those of Africa?
But my question: why so many variations
of accident, illness, act of God,
the grammar of conception gone awry?

For echoing my brother across the centuries:
You're just mad
because you know I'm right.

For asserting that more life is conceived
than can be answered.

Horse Latitudes

No movement, and what's worse: I'm miles
from water. I wake each morning and take my place

on the X. The sheers at the window
flags of surrender.

Who ever heard of a song with no notes, all rests?

I've only now come to accept my position—
a kind of metaphysical widow's walk,

perch from which I strain for the tip of a sail,
a measure of breeze.

Grief and Geometry

If I plotted grief on an xy-plane where
x and y equal time and loss,
$x=3$, $y=-3$, then flipped that point
over the x-axis, y-axis, then
x again, I'd have a perfect
square, four datapoints for each
miscarriage.

Or plot those four points in the night sky,
make my own constellation
(the way the Greeks could dream
up any picture with all those
random stars), The Great Bear,
Leida, Grief Major,
Grief Minor—

What kind of animal or myth would it be?
Winged horse, archer, dove?

But constellations are only
invented by farmers as a memory
aid for planting.

In school I learned the calendar,
how people kept track of time
with notches carved in bone,
memorized star-rise and star-set.

Grief would have to be a bird
that can depart and return
with a soft shudder of feathers.
Bright stars for the tips of wings

and for the eyes I'd choose two
O stars, like those children's eyes—
brightest, bluest,
shortest-lived.

Primer

Held to the light, scrutinized like a prism,
you expect the world to break
into spectacle, spectrum of
grief. Of songs. Memory, recitation,
contradiction. Acorn before
it towers as oak. Not
this obvious paper and ink having
so little to do with you. Sure,
you take in a birth or two, a theory
halfway through of plate tectonics,
but you know the thick milk of mourning
can't stick to the page. It pools.
Its steam rises behind you.

What Is Still, What Is Moving

Vermeer's Woman in Blue Reading a Letter

Apparently nothing moves: the map on the wall, the brass-tacked blue chairs,
the solid mass of table, of woman. Her gaze fixed as ink, as the attitude
of light, fixed as the hinges of the door we cannot see, though if you fast forward

as in time-lapse photography, it is the woman who will
move, close the letter then pull the shutter against street clatter
of wagons and vendors of bread and then sleep. Her man will
or will not come, laden with pepper and nutmeg from the East,

sugar from the West Indies, with stories, perhaps. Mornings she will open
or close the window; nights, take her hair down. There is light
and dark and light again. The child will be born, the map on the wall
bleed its boundaries. Eventually, she shuts her eyes

for good and the walls are the same, but the room is
peopled differently, like the houses I read about
in Amsterdam's Herengracht, or Gentlemen's Canal, where, it was
bragged, one could trace the lineage

for hundreds of years: a succession of merchants,
doctors, diamond cutters, confectioners, and politicians.
The woman, if she is fortunate, carries on
her lineage, too. The letter has its lineage

among letters. But for this post-plague, pre-Napoleonic instant, we allow
her to be without the world, to occupy this narrative
where everything hinges on her desire to read that next word.

Catalog III.

The Classification of Impermanence

for Luke Howard (1772–1864)

Luke Howard was the English amateur meteorologist who devised the classification system for clouds.

To name what is happening even as it slips away,

to classify the many ways breath

crystallizes in winter (against moustache, beard, or scarf), or the many variations

of fog (morning, sea, city).

                          At least with clouds he moved beyond horse tails, elephants
(if he had even seen an elephant),

towers and castles, rhymes for sailors,

to cirrus (Latin for curl of hair), stratus (layer), cumulus (heap),

nimbus: a cloud aspiring to hail or rain.

His task involved his going outside every day, waiting and cloud gazing,
watercolor painting, noticing patterns

the way he had always noticed patterns

in lace, in doilies, in frost climbing like ivy on windows, all of which was to give him

a language to speak theories of rain, to say what he expects

or sees or thinks he sees but which doesn't stay and may not even exist

twenty miles away. And even so, he has faith

in words to limit and pin down the indefinite, the intangible,

the unattainable—to hold fast.

The Second Son

He knows what water knows,
his head passing through my body
like runoff from a storm seeking least resistance.
My muscles and ligaments go back
to their earliest angles, back
to the path of my first son
who mapped the route.

The second son follows as a bird
the inner landmarks of bone,
ribs flexing like saplings, his legs seagrass
under the movement of tides.
He enters the world in phases, a shy moon,
his skull an echo of my geography,
his ears delicate teacups.

He knows how to curl up,
how to root, close his eyes
against the fickleness of light,

what is yet to be heard,
what felt,

voices that clap and peal like bells,
knot of hunger,

fists clenched for the journey.

Braids

Passing the park, the little girls with long hair, gold
running through like Rapunzel's: I long to braid it.
I wanted mine braided as a girl, but

my mother never did. I was always
undone. The smoothness and evenness
of the braid say something

about the care of the person doing the braiding, say
my husband, who after eight years
of marriage tries for the first time to section

my curls into thirds, telling me
he's only done this once before,
growing up on the farm, making rope

on a machine in the barn
to bind the hay bales.
What will my clumsy braid hold together?

He doesn't know when to pull tight, how to hold what's
just been accomplished. Doesn't have a way to bind
the end. I stare at it in the mirror—a far cry

from my college friend's, her braid
past her hip. She'd never cut
her hair. She'd rather

amputate a limb. Now I'm
done with being undone. All braids speak to me
of wanting, textured like

tongues. All tight to control the wanting.
I want to be bounded, moored, to be in relation to, to be
that middle piece winding through.

I read that wisdom lies in knowing
when to hold on, when to let go. We have
two sons. We suppose there'll

be no daughters.

Ballast

Cobblestones are obvious, as is sand.
Water is a surprise—same

element used to stabilize
that may also cause a ship

to capsize. But what about ballast more intangible
than steel, pig iron or lead? Nouns more abstract

than water? Take the man who paces
the deck or the streets

reciting his Latin motto:
Aspirat primo fortuna labori.

Fortune smiles upon our first effort.
Or the woman who carries an umbrella

despite no forecast of rain. Anything
to reduce stress on the skull.

What carries you over these
3,000 fathoms of water other than this

visceral boat? Does anyone admit
to the imagined interaction, or conversation,

which acts as a handrail
in a storm? Or mannerisms—

how a man folds and unfolds his gloves, fiddles
with coins in his pocket. Figments, really:

our steel-hulled wills.
Those words: *talisman, amulet.*

Anything to stave off
salt water in the lungs.

Still Life

In French: *nature morte*, dead nature.
An invitation or a warning?
Perhaps this genre of painting
should be titled Short Life in honor of mortality,
small opportunity we have to breathe, the meal
half eaten or never to be eaten.

Grapes swelled to the size of a newborn's heart,
peaches, plums always on the cusp
of spoiling: this isn't someone's supper, more like
Pompeii, everyone up and left
the table mid-meal, mid-sentence—

Someone had to polish the silver,
pour the wine. The fruit, the objects
like stand-ins for actors in a morality play,
those peaches the twins
Desire, Temptation,
the oysters Lust, skulls or flies always equal
Death, a candle, Time,
Night (the moth) and Day (the butterfly).

How easily the knife pierces the plum.
All angles and questions at once, echo
of the abandoned dinner party. You find your way
around the painting on hairpin
curves, transparent arc of the bottle,
confines of the glass, the simple geometry
of the platter tilted up for an intimate
perspective. And if the painting could speak:
See this table, this world spread out before you—
how close to the edge it all lies.

My Grandmother Peels Apples for Sauce

She cups the apple in her left hand, works
the blade with her right,
thumbs so callused they won't bleed
if she nicks them.
A spiral of peel sighs
into the sink.

In this room, everything is used up:
the vinyl floor—its unglued seam—
frayed holes in her canvas sneakers,
the wallpaper with its orchard
of preserved pears.

She's trained herself
for seven decades
not to want.

When I ask for a bite, it's the peel she allows—
the pots on the stove
waiting, open-mouthed.

Why We Speak English

Because when you say *cup* and *spoon*
your mouth moves the same way as your grandfather's
and his grandfather's before him.
It's Newton's first law: A person in motion
tends to stay in motion with the same speed
and direction unless acted upon by an unbalanced force—
scarcity or greed.
Is there a word for greed in every language?

Because the ear first heard
dyes furs pepper ginger tobacco cotton timber
silk freedom horizon
and the tongue wanted to taste
all these fine things.

And when my son asks why his father speaks Danish
and he and I speak English and Carlos—
at kindergarten—speaks Portuguese:

because Denmark is and has always been.
Our ancestors tracked north and Carlos'
tracked south. What's left in their wake
is language.

Because it comes down
to want, to latitude and longitude as ways to measure
desire, invisible mover of ships—
great clockwise gyre of water in the sea—
like some amusement park ride where boats seem to sail
but run on tracks under the water.

Because to change course now would be like diverting
the Arno, this centuries-long rut we've dug ourselves
into, and how would it be to wake up one morning
with bird *oiseau* or another word entirely?

The Quick of Things

The day my four-year-old
learned to ride a bike, no training wheels,
moving away from me
for the first time
on his own momentum,

I felt this slipping forward—
as if the minute hand on my watch skipped ahead,
cheated the hour.

So starts this pattern of lines like a geometry
proof: I'm point A and he's point B,
moving away from, returning to.

It doesn't take a fortune teller to predict
his leaving: his too-short pants, the bridge
of his nose forming, every day
five new words collect at his feet. He'll disappear
into the quick of things,
a mosaic of backpacks at the school bus stop, a throng
of brown-haired children. All the future days gather
like worry behind a dam.

It ends with me: the lone point
on the circle,
and I'll wait for him like I wait
for the change of seasons,
stake the garden, stack the dishes.

For now he traces circle
after nested circle in the cul-de-sac,
his feet sure on the pedals, this other world
bearing down.

Selling Skies at the Soho Bazaar, 1790

"When I was a boy I used to lie for hours on my back watching the skies, and then go home and paint them; and there was a stall in Soho Bazaar where they sold drawing materials and they used to buy my skies."

—J.M.W. Turner (1775–1851)

Skies appeal to those who aren't satisfied with the three-dimensionality
of furniture, the practicality of pewter tankards
or wooden spoons, who like their landscapes ever-changing or else
frozen in a state of dramatic expectation: a tinge of pink on the forewall
of cumulous. Storms fetch
the highest prices, especially those involving ships or small boats at sea—
almost all heaven and not a lot of middle ground—
everyone wants to see if the boats will be saved,
everyone believes the boats represent a smorgasbord of things:
our lives, mortality, man versus nature.

                        The one thing you can't buy
is time. And so the choice becomes almost comical: sunset
or hairpin? Vapor of fog through which almost
nothing can be discerned except intensity of light? A bit
of confection?

Fast forward 200 years—these are the same people who
purchase mood rings, adopt a star or a planet, who like to be
associated with beauty that can't be owned. Though this isn't
a con, like selling oceanfront property in Kansas.
There is something tangible here, in these interpretations of mist,
clouds that can be pinned to a wall. There is a lady
who keeps returning to the stall for the paintings that promise
rain, each successive set of canvases closer and closer
approximations to the truth.

At Forty

Pattern or absence of pattern, the way a jet flies
into blankness
yet leaves a clear trail, I expect time
to reveal an underdrawing,
hatching of shadows, some rough plan
visible through another spectrum of light.

      Once, at an ophthalmologist's office,
through an accident of mirrors, I saw the interior
of my own eye, the retina's
veins like roots or a web, and then again

ten years later, this time in an astronomy
book—galaxies, clusters of galaxies, superclusters
of galaxies strung out
strands of a cosmic web, the redness
of that image, the light extending like roots
13 billion years in every direction.

      Michelangelo could see a figure
in a block of stone, waiting to be freed.
I want his vision when I look in a mirror,
his mathematical principles for depicting space,
his ability to translate three dimensions into stone.
First I'm in two dimensions, a photograph
glued to the glass; then three—I'm somewhere between
the glass and the background. All my houses, friends
come and gone. How would he sculpt me? How far out
of the stone have I come?

Darwin's Twin Sister

We'll call her Clara. She has an equally keen mind, shares his love of dogs and his weak stomach. She, too, jumps at the chance to voyage on the *Beagle*. On Galapagos, while Charles shoots mocking-thrushes, becomes obsessed with gradations in the size of finches' beaks, she notices how the crew seek shade at the midpoint of the day, sharpen their knives in the best light; how the tortoises travel methodically along well-chosen tracks, hiss and draw in their heads when star-tled; the lack of frogs and how suited they would be to the damp upper woods. She spots not only lineage but will, the staying up late at night to care for the injured. She encodes her thoughts in colors of thread. She's left carrying it all in her head, forced to convey the information through song and lyric. She teaches a bit to the morning glory and to the wren. A measure to the sparrow, the cricket. Some of it survives. Buried in rock, in sand. If you listen, each species takes a part. It's up to you to piece it together.

Sugar in Space

Scientists have discovered glycolaldehyde, a molecular cousin to table sugar, in an interstellar molecular cloud.

So the nursery rhyme was half right: we are made of sugar.
Our backbones. Our hair.

$C_2H_4O_2$, an 8-atom molecule until it links
to other atoms, combines to glucose, ribose,
nucleic acid such as DNA.

I don't know about prebiotic or theoretical chemistry,
but the lesson we should take away
is that our interstellar molecular cousins beget

radio waves, and each molecule, turning end over end,
changing energy states like a wave of bad REM sleep,
has its call, a radio frequency fingerprint.

                                Imagine the signals we send out
on our bad or good days: the days you are lost
and backtracking who knows where on obtuse roads
(impossible to be lost as long as gravity keeps its grip
on the planet,

but in theory, or figuratively: yes).
Or the day you watch your son
being born.

All this agonizing over theories and origins and it comes
down to something small: the sugar bowl
on the table. *Dust to dust*

is partially right, though our forefathers omitted the bit
about interstellar molecular recycling. Impossible
to be nothing.

No wonder soliloquies invoke the night sky.

On Reading about the Illness and Death of Darwin's Daughter Annie

When orthodox medicine fails, Darwin turns to
a dessert spoon of white wine every hour,
sea bathing, mustard poultices, gargle of sulfate
of aluminum and potassium. He packs the patient in damp towels—
anything to shock the body into
fighting, settle the coughs into submission.

He reads her *Genevieve*, the story of a poor village woman in the Alps.

On good days, Annie rides a pony. In the only photo, she wears a gingham dress
and has her braids pinned up by her ears.

He takes notes. This excruciating log of his, her days chronicled
with *well almost very, well not quite, poorly a little, poorly,*
and her nights: *wakeful, good, good not quite.*

The problem is how to distinguish pattern: treatment
and cure, as when
I visited the acupuncturist and he looked
at my tongue and said *too much cold in the uterus*, then
handed me a brown bag of herbs that looked like they had been swept from under
the fall trees; I took evening primrose oil, black cohosh,
false unicorn root, and kept my log:

Day 38: Few cramps
Day 39: Still no signs of bleeding

It's said Darwin had a sinking feeling
at the beginning of the *Beagle's* journey. Imagine his helplessness
at Annie's death. How he loses himself in his work. To his
surviving children he gives a handful of shells
from the voyage, shells he cannot identify.

A Way with Words

Lately, I see language through the wrong end of a telescope; a distant figure on a hillside, walking away; not a child but reduced to the size of a child. Left me with a pocket of words like five scant beans. I used to know *remonstrate, peremptory, emolument*; I can't read Hawthorne now without a dictionary. I recycle syllables like a wilted mantra: *Keep your feet off the couch. Keep your feet off your brother. No going outside with bare feet.* You see what I mean, what I've painted myself into. The fences I construct with language. It wasn't always this way, filing synonyms away like socks in a drawer. Which five words do I teach to my children—*work, pinnacle, feather, root, love*? How to grow back a world from five dried beans? If I'm to start over, where is the manual that tells me under which sign of the zodiac to plant, how deep to furrow, and where—even—is the garden?

Dickinsonia

a Precambrian fossil from 550 million years ago

No fortress of bone or saddleback shell, no venomous fangs,
no antlers or horn. There's something about soft tissues

that begs empathy & forgiveness. The animated creature on screen
navigates the cartoon Precambrian seas. Muck-brown,

ribbed oval disc of a body, no appendages,
no language & no language to describe it

but simile: Worm? Sponge? Plant or animal?
It's like fill-in-the-blank because we can't say exactly.

The smallest the size of an infant's outstretched hand,
the largest that of a man's body. He? She?

With what do we identify? The not knowing
where one belongs? Lack of defenses?

Perhaps it's the Dickinsonia's continual need to feed,
resting place to resting place,

externally digesting the microbial matground through the sole.
To move with no limbs, fins, or tail.

To feed with no mouth. No mouth = no satisfaction
for this creature that survives by taking the world in

with its whole body. Before trees, insects & land
vertebrates, how silent the land must have been:

no body to hold on to
& the rocks having the last word.

Notes and Sources

Source materials for certain poems should be attributed as follows:

—"A Catalog of What We're Not Meant to See," based on information from Robert Hooke's *Micrographia (1665)* (online), Project Gutenberg. The epigraph is from John Banville, "Beauty, Charm, and Strangeness: Science as Metaphor," *Science* 3 (online), July 1998.

—"Isaac Newton Waits Out the Plague," epigraph based on information from the biography of Isaac Newton by Dr. Robert A. Hatch, University of Florida, from the website Luminarium. Online.

—"Wilson's Warbler," epigraph from the biography of Alexander Wilson available at the website *Alexander Wilson, American Ornithologist*, created by Janet Haven and published by the American Studies Program of the University of Virginia. Italicized words quoted or adapted are from the same source. <http://xroads. virginia.edu/~public/wilson/front.html>.

—"*The Mier Expedition: The Drawing of the Black Bean* by Frederic Remington (1896)," epigraph based on information from Joseph Milton Nance, "MIER EXPEDITION," *Handbook of Texas Online* <http://www.tshaonline.org/ handbook/online/articles/qym02>, accessed 2005. Published by the Texas State Historical Association. Art referenced: Frederic S. Remington. *The Mier Expedition: The Drawing of the Black Bean*, c. 1896. Oil on canvas. The Museum of Fine Arts, Houston.

—"After Seven Months, Alaskans Begin to Bury Their Dead," based on information from Matt Volz, "Springs softens the ground, so Alaskans bury the dead," *Laredo Morning Times* (online), May 10, 2004.

—"A Brief History of Passenger Pigeon," based on information from "The Passenger Pigeon," *Smithsonian Encyclopedia* (online), 3/01 revised.

—"Platypus:Hoax," epigraph from George Shaw, *The naturalist's miscellany*— *Platypus Anatinus*, June 1799 / London: F. P. Nodder, [1813 or 1814] Vol. 10. Inspiration from the history of the platypus website <http://www.platypus.org. uk/facts-history.htm>. July 2013 and Neil Shubin's *Your Inner Fish*. New York: Vintage, 2009.

—"Found Poem: Sir Hamond L'Estrange Gives the Only Documented Account of a Living Dodo in Britain, 1638," Sir Hamond L'Estrange quotations from Steve Connor's "Driven to extinction: Who killed the Dodo?" *The Independent* (online), 9 June 2006.

—"What the Frog's Eye Tells the Frog's Brain," italicized lines from a course in Practical Thinking (online), The Open University, 2004.

—"Selling Skies at the Soho Bazaar, 1790," the epigraph is from Jan Marsh, "Pigments of the imagination," *The Independent*, 28 June 1997. Online.

— "Darwin's Twin Sister" based on information from Charles Darwin's *The Voyage of the Beagle*. Vol. XXIX. The Harvard Classics. New York: P. F. Collier & Son, 1909–14; Bartleby.com, 2001. www.bartleby.com/29/17.html. [3/29/15].

—"Sugar in Space," based on information from "Sugar in Space," *NASA Science News* (online), June 20, 2000.

—"On Reading about the Illness and Death of Darwin's Daughter Annie," italicized lines from Randal Keynes' *Darwin, His Daughter, and Human Evolution.* New York: Riverhead Books, 2001.

—"Dickinsonia," based on information from "Australia: Awakening." *NOVA*. PBS. 4/10/13 and Michael Anissimov's "What is Dickinsonia?" (online), wiseGEEK. 11/19/13.